W9-CQL-130

Japan

World Partners

Japan

Christopher Meeks

The Rourke Corporation, Inc.

To Carol,
a fabulous writer and editor,
with many thanks.

Copyright 1990 by The Rourke Corporation, Inc.

All rights reserved. No part of this book may be reproduced, or utilized in any form or by any means, electronic or mechanical, including photocopying, recording or by any information storage and retrieval system without permission from the publisher.

The Rourke Corporation, Inc.
P.O. Box 3328, Vero Beach, FL 32964

Meeks, Christopher.
    Japan / by Christopher Meeks.
        p.   cm. — (World partners)
    Includes bibliographical references and index.
    Summary: Explores Japan's culture and its economy today—a productive and efficient one which has grown out of the devastation of World War II and thrown Japan into an interdependent partnership with the United States and made it a world economic force.
        ISBN 0-86593-089-9
        1. Japan—Juvenile literature. 2. Japan—Foreign economic relations—Juvenile literature 3. Japan—Foreign relations—1945—Juvenile literature. [1. Japan. 2. Japan—Foreign economic relations.] I. Title II. Series.
DS806.M42   1990
952.04—dc20   90-8739
                                                 CIP
                                               AC

Series Editor: Gregory Lee
Editors: Elizabeth Sirimarco and Marguerite Aronowitz
Book design and production: The Creative Spark, Capistrano Beach, CA
Cover photograph: Steve Elmore/Tom Stack & Associates

Japan

Table of Contents

1 Economic Superpower

Japan is a country that puzzles many Americans. A very small country—the size of Montana—Japan is so mountainous that only 37 percent of the country can be farmed or lived in. Japan's population, however, is 125 million people, or about half that of the United States. Imagine half of America living in one-third of Montana and you have some idea of how crowded Japan is.

Japan churns out 10 percent of the world's goods. Despite its small size, Japan's economy is second only to the United States in the world. Japan makes and exports so many things that almost all nations depend on Japan for many of their needs.

What also puzzles Americans is the way Japanese think and act. Their culture emphasizes what the Japanese call *wa*. Wa is a sense of team spirit that promotes the interest of the group or family above that of the individual. Americans cannot understand a people who suppress their own needs or desires and exist only to please their boss or family. Despite their differences, however, Japan and the United States have strong ties. They are world partners.

In World War II, Japan was our bitter enemy. We hit Japan with 90,000 tons of conventional

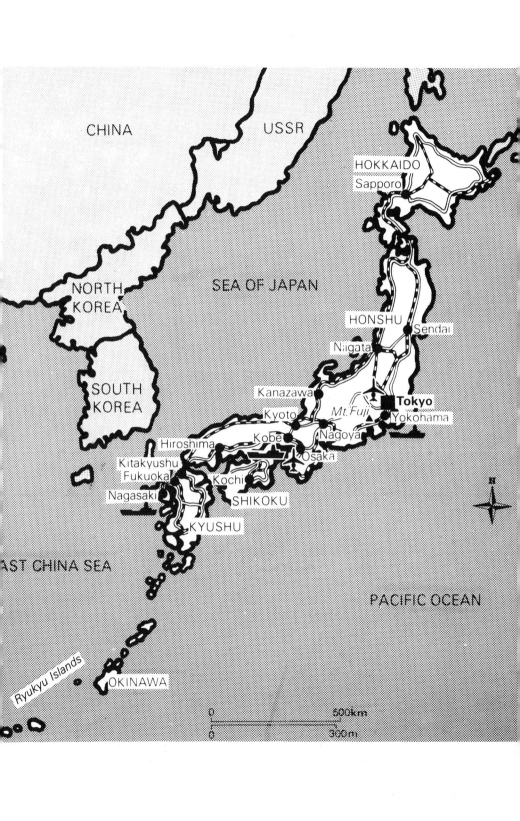

and fire-producing bombs and two nuclear blasts before the Japanese surrendered. Japan's major cities were leveled. The country and economy were in ruins.

Today, Japan—a small country that has the most efficient and productive economy in the world— is one of America's major allies. Their incredible turnaround from poverty to riches, from enemy to friend, has produced what former president Ronald Reagan called, "the most important bilateral relationship the United States has with any country in the world."

This book will explore that relationship. We will examine the reasons why Japan is so important in the world today. Then we will compare this economic superpower to the United States.

From Rubble To Renaissance

A country made up of four main islands and many smaller ones, Japan sits in the Pacific Ocean just east of China and Korea, and south of Siberia in the Soviet Union. The name Japan, in fact, derives from the Chinese phrase meaning "the source of the sun," and describes the country's geographical position east of China.

In World War II, Japan pushed its empire outward like a balloon that grew bigger and bigger in a quest for more territory to conquer. At its peak, the Japanese empire included the Philippine Islands, Vietnam, Korea, Thailand, Burma, Manchuria, parts of China, Sumatra, Java, hundreds of Pacific islands, and half of New Guinea.

In 1941, Japan attacked Pearl Harbor in Hawaii, and America jumped into the war against Japan. Through constant aerial bombing, American forces leveled every major Japanese city except Kyoto by 1945. Americans landed on Okinawa, a main military base. After Germany had surrendered, President Truman gave the military per-

mission to use the newly developed atomic bomb on Japan, hoping its terrible destruction would cause Japan to surrender quickly.

After two atomic blasts, one on Hiroshima and one on Nagasaki, Japan surrendered. The date was August 15, 1945. In a radio broadcast, Emperor Hirohito told his people that they must "endure the unendurable and suffer the insufferable" of an American occupation. On August 30, General Douglas MacArthur landed near Tokyo and began the task of reorganizing and rebuilding a devastated country.

Recovery

Today, Japan has not only recovered, but for over 25 consecutive years it has had an annual *trade surplus* with the United States. This means the United States buys many more items from Japan than Japan buys from the U.S., thus mak-

Paper lanterns are set afloat down Hiroshima's Motoyasu River to honor the victims of history's first atomic bombing. The gutted dome building in the background was left standing after World War II as a memorial.

Japanese History

Japanese history has been rich and diverse. Like all cultures, their past is filled with great triumphs and great defeats, cultural advancement and desolation. The time line below gives a general view of Japan since 552 A.D.

Archaic Period *(Before 552 A.D.)*
Migration to Japan of peoples from the mainland, ranging from Manchuria to Southeast Asia. By the fourth century, the country becomes partially unified.

Asuka Period *(552-710)*
Buddhism arrives in Japan from China by way of Korea. The religion strongly influences the arts.

Nara Period *(710-794)*
The first permanent capital is built at Nara. Chinese culture has been a strong influence in Japan for several centuries.

Heian Period *(794-1185)*
Japan begins to sever its ties with the mainland. The capital is moved to a new city near Nara called Heian-kyo (now Kyoto). Japanese Buddhism develops its own distinct character. Power shifts from the Emperor to the Fujiwara family. In the provinces, powerful warrior families lead to the development of a military class, the samurai.

Kamakura Period *(1185-1333)*
The samurai Minamota Yoritomo defeats a rival and establishes the first military government, or shogunate, *at Kamakura. This form of government lasts until 1867. The Imperial court stays in Kyoto. Its influence is weak. Mongols try and fail to take Japan but defending Japan costs a great deal and leads to collapse of the Kamakura shogunate.*

Japanese History

Muromachi Period *(1333-1568)*
Time is marked by warfare between strong families and, occasionally, by the existence of more than one emperor. The capital returns to Kyoto. The tea ceremony is developed. A worldly Shinto belief arose. St. Francis Xavier, a missionary priest, arrives in 1549 and introduces Christianity.

Azuchi-Momoyama Period *(1568-1600)*
Political unification is initiated by Oda Nobunaga and achieved by Toyotomi Hideyoshi in 1590. Invasions into Korea prove costly and bring collapse of Hideyoshi regime.

Edo or Tokugawa Period *(1600-1868)*
Tokugawa Ieyasu moves the government to Edo. His shogunate embarks on a policy of isolation that persecutes Christian converts, ejects all Europeans, and does not allow the Japanese to leave the country. Peace reigns for the first time in several hundred years. Isolation ends with the arrival of Admiral Perry in 1853.

Meiji Period *(1868-1912)*
Under Emperor Meiji, imperial power returns and modernization occurs rapidly. Fact-finding missions are enacted throughout the Western world for new ideas and technology. Japan embarks on an imperialist drive that leads to war and victory against China (1894-1895) and Russia (1904-1905) and the annexation of Korea (1909).

Taisho and Showa Periods *(1912-present)*
Expansionism leads Japan to capture much of Asia. By bombing Pearl Harbor, the Japanese bring American hostilities. They are defeated in 1945. The Allies give their country a new constitution and help rebuild the country. Japan becomes a major economic force in the world.

ing Japan one of the most influential countries in the world. How did this amazing and quick transformation occur?

First, occupation officials (those who helped administer Japan's recovery) drafted and implemented a new Japanese constitution whose basic purpose, from an American point of view, was to make sure that Japan would "not become a menace to the United States or to the peace and security of the world." Also, the forces wanted to establish "a peaceful and responsible government"—a democracy.

American occupational forces guided the new Japanese government for the next five years. A number of major changes were made during this period. Ownership of cultivated land was transferred from landlord to tenant farmer. Everyone was given voting privileges, including women, and equal rights were stressed. An educational system much like that in the United States was started. Wartime leaders were taken from their posts, ultra-nationalist organizations were dissolved, and monopolies of power in business and finance were broken up.

These reforms changed Japanese society greatly and affected their culture. No longer did only a small percentage of people and companies own and command the most power. These new freedoms unleashed powerful new economic forces.

Hiroshi Takeuchi of the Long Term Credit Bank of Japan said, "If Japan had not gone to war or if it had negotiated an end to the war, thus avoiding an occupation, Japan's economy today might have reached the level of, perhaps, South Korea's. Japan's workers, like those in South Korea under authoritarian rule, most likely would still be diligently putting in six-day, 66-hour work weeks, earning low wages."

Instead, the economy exploded into growth of

between 8 percent and 14 percent every year from 1959 to 1974. Such small companies as Honda and Sony flourished. Land reform not only raised agricultural productivity but also gave purchasing power to people who had never had it before.

Where education had once been only for the elite, now everyone could go to school. Today 90 percent of all boys and 91 percent of all girls graduate from high school. Virtually all citizens can read, and 93 percent of all Japanese subscribe to at least one of the country's 125 daily newspapers.

Japan's industries grew into global giants. In many markets—textiles, steel, cars, computers, semiconductors, robots—Japanese products are of excellent quality and improving relentlessly. Only in space exploration and airplane manufacturing does the U.S. hold a world lead, but even that is shrinking as Japan aims for the top spot in those markets.

The incredible growth of Japan's economy has had a tremendous effect on the nation's people. They have become major investors around the world, either lending money to projects or simply buying goods and foreign property outright. In fact, a popular joke in America sprang up after Japanese Prime Minister Toshiki Kaifu visited President Bush in 1990 to discuss the trade of products between both countries. In the joke, Bush says to Kaifu, "You've got to buy more American goods." Kaifu replies, "Fine. I'll take Los Angeles."

Japan's wealth has had some peculiar side effects. For example, in 1989 the cost of a golf membership in that country was $206,000. Dr. Michael Tuck, a Los Angeles medical researcher, went to dinner with a group of people to a pleasant but not exclusive restaurant. The bill for 18 people came to $18,000, and the Japanese host

added a $2,000 tip.

Such luxuries as golfing and elegant dining have zoomed beyond the reach of the average Japanese, who makes a modest living—a little below that of the average American. Only those who can charge expensive, leisurely pleasures to their business can afford them.

Real estate, too, has climbed far beyond the reach of most Japanese. A prime site in Tokyo in 1989 sold for $269,000 a square meter, which is roughly the size of a bath towel. On the average, land in Japan—a scarce commodity in an over-crowded and mountainous country—is 100 times more expensive than land in the United States. The total value of all the land in Japan is more than four times the value of all the land in America, even though Japan has only one fifty-seventh as much land suitable for housing as the United States.

Such high prices, combined with average wages, have caused social inequality. A modest home on the outskirts of Tokyo will sell for $2 million and up. So most people must resign themselves to a lifetime of renting, and even that is expensive. The average city-dwelling couple typically shares a tiny, two-room, 400-square-foot apartment which includes kitchen area, bath-room and roll-up bedding mats for sleeping on the floor.

Economic Factors

Why is Japan doing so well as a country if its citizens are only doing modestly? In addition to their efficient factories, one economic factor often cited is the Japanese habit of saving money. On the whole, the Japanese save 20 percent of their pre-tax income, while Americans save only a lit-tle more than five percent. Americans are some of the worst savers in the world. Japanese banks have access to a large fund of capital to invest (from its savers), while American banks do not have such ready capital. Savings help make an economy strong.

Another factor in Japan's economic strength is its small defense budget. The American govern-ment spends just over 5 percent of its overall budget on defense, while the Japanese spend just 1 percent, limited by law. The difference in bil-lions of dollars is staggering. The Japanese, therefore, have more money to spend on social problems than Americans, making for a more

The late Emperor Hirohito was a prominent world figure prior to World War II. After the Japanese surrender he became a figurehead stripped of power.

well-off society in Japan.

This difference in the defense budgets, however, can be blamed on America and its allies when they negotiated Japan's surrender after World War II. They did not want to see Japan strongly armed again, so Article 9 of the "peace constitution" reads:

Aspiring sincerely to an international peace based upon justice and order, the Japanese people forever renounce war as a sovereign right of the nation and the threat or use of force as a means of settling international disputes.... Land, sea and air forces, as well as other war potential, will never be maintained.

America, therefore, took on the responsibility of defending Japan, and has that responsiblity to this day. The Japanese themselves have put controls on their defense projects. In 1976, a new law fixed their defense costs at one percent of the national budget. An international debate has begun on whether the Japanese should help pay for their defense.

Economists predict that by the year 2000, Japan will surpass America in *per capita* personal income. As a nation, their economy very well may lead the world.

2 Japanese Art And Ideology

One amazing thing about human beings is how different they can be from one another. Not only do people come in different shapes, sizes and colors, but their minds can work in many ways. No one way is necessarily the "right" way.

Think, for instance, about how a boy might argue with his father. Say they are arguing about eating. The son is not hungry and does not want to eat. The father, seeing that it is six o'clock, insists it is dinner time. Each person feels he is "right" and the other person is "wrong."

In fact, they each may be right in their own way. The son is right in that he is not hungry right now. So why eat? The father is right because he knows his son must eat to grow, and that he always gets hungry once he sees food.

Much in the same way that two individuals can think differently, whole countries—because of their different cultures—can have different attitudes. Each country can be "right" in its own way.

Culture includes everything that socially transmits behavior: the kinds of beliefs people have, the art they make, the government they have, and the food they like. Culture is also the furniture they use, the kinds of houses and

apartments they live in, the language they speak, and much more. All people are shaped a great deal by their environment and by other people.

▲

A familiar scene: a family watching television at home.

The best way to see how another country can be so different and think so uniquely is to travel there—see, hear, taste, touch and smell the differences. For instance, one can smell flowers blooming in the Netherlands or bread baking in India. See the majestic Alps in Switzerland. Taste curried goat in Jamaica or raw fish in Japan. Hear a tuba concert in Germany or gamelan music in Java. Touch statues in Argentina or white beach sand in Morocco.

To get a glimpse of Japanese thinking, and get an idea how and why Japan came to be such an important player in the world, let's take a brief look at Japanese culture.

Cultural History

Japan is composed of four main islands and a group of smaller ones, while the United States has a huge and continuous land mass (except for Alaska and Hawaii). These two distinctions alone have shaped differences in culture.

In America's past, settlers from many different countries spent decades pushing west, exploring and starting cities. We formed what some people call a "pioneer ethic," meaning our thinking— even today—tends toward exploration and building. (The television show *Star Trek* takes the pioneer ethic to outer space where we "boldly go where no man has gone before.")

Japan, on the other hand, does not have in its history a forging of a new land or a mixing of people from many other countries. They have always had their islands and have kept pretty much to themselves. In Japanese history centuries have gone by when no one from other countries was permitted in. Because Japan is located far off the mainland, this was easy to do.

At other times (the 7th and 8th centuries, the 15th and 16th centuries, and from 1868 to the present day) Japan has been quite interested in other countries. The Japanese have borrowed bits and pieces of other cultures and made them their own. For instance, Buddhism and *kanji*, a system of brushstroke writing which has over 50,000 characters, came from China; *besuboru*, or baseball, which the Japanese play with a passion, came from America.

Art As A Way Of Life

In art, the Japanese are particularly concerned with highly aesthetic and emotive forms, and not so much with philosophies. "Harmony is to be valued," said the influential 7th-century royal art patron Shotoku Taishi. This concept, more than anything else, lies at the heart of Japanese culture.

Because they live in a crowded, mostly urban environment, the Japanese not surprisingly have chosen to emphasize restraint and contemplation in both art and architecture. Even so, they make room for beauty in hundreds of small ways. They preserve and cherish the past. Their temples, shrines and gardens in a few of the unbombed cities such as Kyoto, for example, go back hundreds of years. The tea ceremony, still widely practiced today, was developed in the 15th century. Japanese history goes back as far as the 4th century. The ability to balance the old and the new derives from their ancient religion, *Shinto*, which emphasizes the natural order of things and advocates the acceptance of that order. Nature is revered. Beauty can be seen in a single leaf.

Fosco Maraini, an Italian writer who teaches Japanese studies, describes Shintoism as a positive, energetic, vital view of the world. "Underlying this faith—even in Tokyo—is a reverence for nature." Nature holds truth, goodness and beauty, and is perfect in its own right. In Japan, he believes, ideas do not necessarily come with two sides as they do in the West. In Western thought, for instance, there is God and man, creator and creature, body and soul, good and evil, natural and supernatural reality, the sacred and the vulgar. "In Shinto, men, the world and the gods all belong to what is essentially a single, vital continuum."

The Japanese have an astoundingly high literacy rate—98 percent, compared to America's 87 percent (which means that in America 13 percent of the adult population cannot read or write). In Japan, reading and writing are major pastimes. More than 40,000 new book titles are published each year. It seems as if nearly everyone writes poetry. At least one million 17-syllable *haiku* poems are printed each year. *Haiku,* though

Tokyo's Yasukuni Shrine, *the Shinto temple honoring Japan's 2.46 million war dead.*

short, are full of imagery and offer much to contemplate. Words are purposely omitted to heighten effect, as in the following poem written by Matsuo Basho, who lived from 1644 to 1694:

> The peaks of clouds
> Have crumbled into fragments—
> The moonlit mountain.

The Japanese tend to forego more hectic pursuits but gain satisfaction from simple things and from humble, solitary pursuits such as gardening. *Ikebana*, the classical art of flower arranging, and *cha-no-yu*, the art of the tea ceremony, are popular. "The sound of wind in a pine and the reflection of a flower petal in a pond's surface are real treasures to a Japanese," wrote one person.

There are three traditional forms of Japanese theatre: *noh*, where there are just two main characters and masks are frequently used; *kabuki*, a lively and colorful theatre with song and dance; and *bunraku* puppet theatre.

Japanese cuisine is marked by elegance and simplicity. "Food should be prepared to do honor to the essence of the materials chosen," one master chef has said. Only the freshest ingredients are used so that one's meal not only tastes good but looks good. A visit to a respectable Japanese restaurant in America will delight a diner with such things as radishes sliced as flowers and food arranged as delicately as a painting.

3 Daily Living

Don't be misled that everyone in Japan is always off in some quiet place contemplating. Television is the most popular form of diversion, with the average family spending eight hours and fifteen minutes each day in front of the set. *Pachinko*, a vertical pinball game where beads fall through rows of nails, serves as a pastime much as video games are popular in America. And hitting a bucket of golf balls is so popular that multi-storied and mechanized driving ranges are found all over Japan.

The Japanese way of relaxing and coping with the pressures of work and modern living appear to be effective. Serious crime in Japan is minimal compared to America. In a recent year in Tokyo, for example, 505 robberies were reported, compared to 100,550 in New York City alone. In one year, handguns killed only 77 people in Japan but 11,522 in the United States. Life expectancy in Japan is longer than in most developed countries. The median age for men is 74 years, and 80 for women. Divorce is only one-quarter of the rate it is in the United States, and unemployment and school dropouts are similarly low.

Language

Much of the way people think is influenced by the structure of their language. The English language places the subject first, then an action, then the object. "I kicked the ball," for example. In Japanese, the word order is different with constructions of the type "by-me-hunted bear" rather than "the bear that I hunted," and "a-singing I went" rather than "I sang as I went." There are few if any conjunctions (words that join phrases together such as "and" and "but"). Meaningful elements are connected to stems, as in "house-my" for "my house" and "house-from" for "from the house."

What does this mean? Americans have a dif-

A familiar American fast food chain serves a typical city lunch crowd.

▲
Besoboru has rapidly become Japan's favorite team sport. Many American baseball stars have signed contracts with Japanese teams.

ferent sequential order in thought processes. Akio Morita, the chairman of Sony, explained the English language to a Japanese audience this way: "It is impossible to interpret in the same sequential order as the thought process that generated the words in Japanese. Thus, when a message is to be delivered, it is regrettable but true, that the sequential thought process of Japanese is in the minority in the world."

Team Spirit

The Japanese tend to view themselves not as important individuals, but rather as members of a group, all striving toward group goals. They downplay personal advancement. The Japanese word *wa* defines them in many aspects of what they do. *Wa* is the sense of team spirit that expects the individual to subordinate everything else in life to make the interests of the group the most important facet in his or her life.

In his book *You Got To Have Wa*, author Robert Whiting looks at the game of *besuboru* (baseball). He compares the way the Japanese and Americans think about the sport and how it affects the game. In spring training, for example, Americans start workouts about five weeks before the season begins, and practice for about four hours a day. The Japanese start three full months ahead of opening day, and practice seven hours a day. In general, more is better for the Japanese.

Japan's major leagues permit two American players on each of their twelve teams. These Americans, who are usually older, fading stars, come to Japan and learn the differences the hard way. "Japanese managers are iron-handed disciplinarians who believe that great players are made, not born, and they try to reshape the foreign players into the Japanese mold. The Americans, intense individualists that they are, rebel. The Japanese conclude that the Americans are rude, lazy, and worse, lacking in...*wa*."

Wa applies to one's company (or baseball team), to one's family, and to one's nation. Whatever individual dreams a person may have are often pushed away to satisfy a role.

This giving up of "self" also helps the Japanese survive modern living. Because Tokyo is so crowded and expensive, many live outside the city and commute for up to four hours a day. Tokyo's subways during rush hour are so crowded that special white-gloved attendants push people into the cars so the doors can close. Train and subway riders accept the crowding and try to relax. "Millions of commuters ride trains as crowded as 19th-century slave ships," a writer once observed, "but show no signs of mutiny. Even with someone's newspaper shoved in their face and someone's elbow jammed in their side, they remain indifferent."

In America there is a saying, "The squeaky

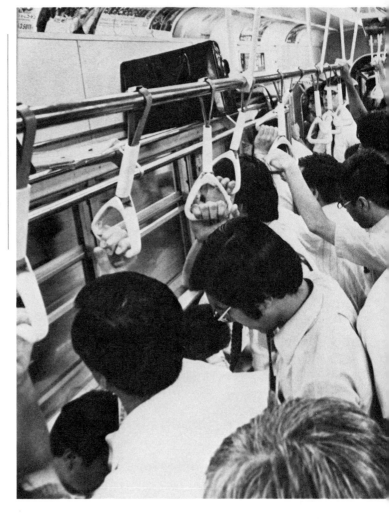

▶

*Rush hour,
Tokyo-style. This
subway car is so
jammed with
commuters that
it's hard to see
the plush seats
and walls free of
graffiti.
Muggings are
nearly unheard of
in Japanese
subways.*

wheel gets the grease." The Japanese also have a saying, "The nail that sticks up gets pounded down."

The Family

After high school or college, most Japanese men get jobs with companies that will employ them for the rest of their lives. Women often marry and raise families while working at least part-time. Forty percent of the work force is made up of women, but only 5.3 percent of Japanese managerial jobs are filled by women.

Despite stereotypes, Japanese homemakers are not subservient *cho-cho san* who follow only their husbands' commands. Instead they are able and tough administrators who run the households and push their children toward excellence. Eight out of 10 *sarariman* (salarymen)—people we call white collar workers—automatically turn their full paychecks over to their wives, who in turn give out allowances and run the family budget.

As one can see, the Japanese outlook, culture and way of thinking are quite unique. With them, the Japanese have helped shape the world.

Japanese-American Trade

In the 1950s, "Made In Japan" meant poor quality. Hammers would bend, toys would break apart, radios would not last. Today "Made in Japan" is a symbol of value. The Japanese not only turn out a large volume of goods, they insist on quality.

So strong is Japanese quality that in 1989, for the first time ever, a Japanese car—the Honda Accord—was the top-selling car in America.

Before 1989, Lee Iacocca, chairman of the American car company Chrysler, used to sell his cars with the slogan, "If you can find a better car, buy it." In 1990, Chrysler's commercials show Iococca talking about Japan, objecting to "the idea that anything made overseas is better than anything made in America."

American economists and political leaders compare our industry and economy to Japan's and worry. The fact is that the small country of Japan, a land with few natural resources, has made a fine art out of quality manufacturing. American business must refocus its efforts on the excellence of its products or see fewer people in America and around the world buying them.

The Trade Imbalance

For years television, newspaper and radio news have been talking about "the trade imbalance with Japan." What is this imbalance and why is it important? To find the answer, we must first look at how economies and international trade work.

In simple terms, a country's economy reflects what goods and services its people make and sell. Jamaica's economy, for example, is dependent on coffee and bananas. That is, many people work at growing coffee and bananas because they are the country's main *exports*. Exports are what a country sells to other countries. In New Zealand, sheep are important because meat and wool are its main exports. Japan's main exports are cars, textiles, steel and many high-technology items such as computers and computer parts,

The Japanese auto industry has become a huge success. These Toyotas are waiting to be loaded onto a container ship for export to the U.S.

Japanese Government

The Japanese parliament, the seat of power, is called the Diet. *While Japan does not have a president, it has a* prime minister, *as does England and many other nations. The prime minister is elected by the House of Representatives from among the members of the Diet, and he can always be replaced by the members. Because of this, he—there has never been a "she"—has less personal power than an American president, and acts more like the head of a committee.*

Nathaniel B. Thayer, a professor of Japanese politics at John Hopkins University, disagrees with the description of Japan's democratic legislature as a "rubber stamp." Because all members of the parliament are chosen in a popular election, says Thayer, the parliament "is more than a rubber stamp. It is what the constitution says it is: the highest organ of state power." It also allows "non-standard" parties to exist, such as two political parties which preach violent revolution. So the political system in Japan gives everyone a chance to express his or her opinion.

VCRs, televisions and robots.

Imports are what a country buys. Jamaica, for instance, does not make any cars, so all of its cars have to be imported. The same goes for New Zealand. Although America makes many cars—Ford, General Motors and Chrysler are our three biggest auto companies—we nonetheless import a large number of cars. Car buyers love to have choices. Foreign cars, which used to represent only a small percentage of cars sold in America, have become more and more popular.

Trade balance (or *imbalance)* refers to how much a country exports versus how much it imports. It can be thought of much like a personal checking account. If you have a job and you put your paycheck in your checking account, then you have money to spend. Your work, in essence, is your export. When you want to buy something, groceries for instance, you then write a check for it. The groceries are your import. If you write more checks than you have money for, you have an imbalance. You will have to export (that is, work) more.

Countries that export more than they import--like Japan or America—are rich compared to countries that import more than they export—like El Salvador or Pakistan.

This is a very simple explanation, because other factors are involved such as efficiency and education. When a country's people are highly educated, they can sell goods and services that are more complex and expensive—which means more money for them to spend.

Efficiency refers to how much effort and expense goes into making something. One country, for instance, might make a "widget" (a mythical item) using one ton of coal and ten people working ten hours. Another country making the same widget might use two tons of coal and 12 people working 12 hours. The first country, therefore, manufactures widgets more efficiently and can probably sell its widgets for a cheaper price.

Japan is often viewed as being a more highly educated and efficient country than America. Many of their goods and services are wanted more often around the world than those of America. Americans buy far more Japanese goods than Japanese people buy American goods. Therefore, there is a trade imbalance. Each year, Japan takes in at least $40 billion more than it spends.

So who cares if there's an imbalance? Americans do, because that $40 billion comes from America. We don't want a large trade imbalance because it weakens the American economy.

Most countries try to make as much money as they can for their own people, and export as much as they can to other countries. Japan happens to be better at doing this than anyone else.

There is much more happening, however, than just people choosing one country's goods over another. For example, some Americans are upset because Japan's market is not as "open" as America's market. This is because Japanese laws and traditions exclude many foreign goods, like rice. Although American rice would be much cheaper if Japan imported it and sold it to its people, the laws in Japan will not allow foreign rice to be imported.

Goods often cost more in Japan than in the United States because of taxes and other pricing policies. Televisions, cars, computers, and VCRs cost less outside of Japan than in Japan. Food is 60 to 70 percent higher there than in the U.S. Steak that is $10 a pound in America is about $18 a pound in Japan. When the Japanese travel—nearly 10 million traveled in 1989—they see how much less expensive it is to buy things elsewhere. The average Japanese traveler brings back

$2,200 worth of foreign goods.

President Bush called Japan's market "unfair" to U.S. goods and wants all trade barriers dropped. He and others feel Japan's market should be as open to America as America's market is open to Japan. But even if Japan drops its trade barriers, will the trade imbalance drop? That's a good question. President Bush and others think so, but the Japanese could choose to buy European or Asian instead of American products. After all, the Japanese trade laws and customs affect the entire world, not just America. Also, in order for American companies to do well in Japan, American companies must be willing to pay for offices, staff and advertising in Japan. With land, buildings, and practically everything so expensive in Japan, will American companies be willing to pay for these higher costs? Only the future will tell.

In 1985, in a special agreement with Japan called the "Plaza Accord," America devalued the

▲
The remarkable "bullet train" that whisks commuters across Japan at high speed.

U.S. dollar and the Japanese yen was strengthened. In other words, the Japanese could get almost twice as many dollars for their yen as before. This should have made American products much more appealing to the Japanese because they would be able to buy more American goods for less money. At the same time, with the yen costing so much more for Americans in an exchange, it would mean that Japanese items would cost more in the United States. This should have made Americans buy fewer Japanese goods, right? This did not happen. Americans still kept buying Japanese products and the Japanese still bought few American goods. The trade imbalance remained much the same.

What this shows, says economist Robert J. Shapiro, is that even with a cheaper dollar, "we are less competitive in our own market because we are less productive than our rivals." Shapiro says that Americans are less productive because they do not spend enough money to develop new technologies and educate and train workers. They don't put forth enough effort to organize the work place and take up new business challenges. In short, Americans will have to do better to remain competitive in the world economy.

The Puzzle Of The Japanese Economy
When the yen was strengthened and the dollar weakened, the trade imbalance should have dropped. It didn't. When stocks and land in Japan rose in value at an astonishing rate (40 percent in one year not too long ago), such skyrocketing prices should have spilled over to the Japanese consumer. But they didn't because *inflation* (the rise in the cost of goods and services over time) remained around three percent, or about half of that in America. When the New York Stock Exchange dropped hundreds of

points in November 1987, stock exchanges all around the world fell sharply. Japan's stock exchange should have fallen as well, but it didn't. Because Japan brings in so much money, the standard of living in Japan should be quite high. It isn't. Why doesn't the Japanese economy work like the American economy?

Since Japanese people have their own way of thinking, we should expect that their economic "rules" will not follow American guidelines. So much about Japan puzzles Americans—its politics, its way of doing business, its culture—that we should look at certain aspects of Japan more closely.

Karel Van Wolferen, author of *The Enigma of Japanese Power*, calls the Japanese economy a "money machine." This is because the Japanese government and large businesses are quite

Japan has shown particular talent in the production of electronics. Here, bargain hunters shop at Akihabara, a Tokyo electronics center.

▲
A New Year's day crowd gathers at Tokyo's Meiji Jingu shinto shrine. They have come to cast money into an offertory box and pray for happiness in the new year.

friendly to each other and work together for the good of the country. Such a close relationship is unique in the world.

Wolferen, who has lived in Japan for the last 25 years, says that Japan's government is so aligned with big business that one cannot call it truly democratic. Politicians, bankers, monetary leaders and executives are linked together in business, and may also be good friends with each other. Because businesses do not have to worry much about government intervention (the parliament is a virtual "rubber stamp" for big business), Japanese corporations can invest in research and development for a much longer time than American companies can afford.

Wolferen also states that Western and Japanese goals are different. "Industrial expansion in the Western democracies aims to make life more livable and to expand choices for consumers." The Japanese in both government and industry, however, tend to view world economics as Japan against the world, and so they strive for domination in as many sectors as possible. They do this at the cost of other desirables in life.

5 New Trends

►

Opposite page, Akio Morita, chairman of Sony Corporation. Morita has attained fame worldwide as a shrewd businessman.

According to an August 1989 poll conduct-ed by *Business Week* and Lou Harris, 68 percent of Americans view the "econom-ic threat from Japan" as a more serious threat to the future of the United States than the military threat from the Soviet Union. The Japanese have not been unaware of or immune to such thinking or the American pressure to change their trade system. While Japanese prime ministers and politicians have been working to change their system with new laws, a Japanese backlash has been forming.

An example of this backlash can be found in a Japanese book called *The Japan That Can Say No*, by Sony chairman Akio Morita and novelist/politician Shintaro Ishihara. The book, while only sold in Japan (and a best-seller there), has been translated into English and photocopied in America for American politicians to read.

The book's premise is that the Japanese tend to be a humble people. They either evade hard questions (they can't say "no"), or they defer to Americans too often. The authors suggest that the Japanese should take their economic power, based on technological and industrial superiori-ty, and use it to back up their "no" when they want to say "no."

While much of what Morita says is tempered and informative, Ishihara's pieces at times become inflammatory, accusing America of racism, false pride and bad management, among other things. He suggests Japan could respond to American criticism by no longer selling the most advanced computer microchips to the United States, but selling them to the Soviet Union instead. (Microchips are used in state-of-the-art military computers.) This reversal, he says, "would upset the entire military balance."

Morita points out some of the reasons for Japan's success and America's economic problems. Industry, Morita says, requires three types of creativity: inventive genius, product-planning-and-production creativity, and creativity in marketing. "The strength in Japanese industry is in finding many ways to turn basic technology into products and using basic technology."

For example, Bell Laboratories in America invented the *transistor*, an electronic device. Although the transistor was invented here, the only use America could find for it was in hearing aids, where the small size was important.

Sony Corporation licensed the transistor patent from Bell Laboratories in 1953, and discovered a new use for the device: small radios. Then they developed a marketing campaign for it based on the idea, "Don't be satisfied with one radio for the whole family, get your own radio." The same marketing strategy was later used for televisions. Transistors eventually replaced the big and inefficient tubes that used to be in radios, televisions, computers and anything "high tech." Today transistors have gotten much smaller and are called *semiconductors*.

Another example of Sony's brilliance in invention and marketing is their Walkman. Before the Walkman stereo (with its ultralight headphones) was manufactured and imported to

Japanese Etiquette

The Japanese have made etiquette (social manners) into a national art. Some of the more common expressions of Japanese manners include:

• Bowing. This is the Japanese equivalent of shaking hands. Bowing indicates respect, and the deeper the bow, the more respect one shows for the other person. Generally, a young person would be expected to bow deeper when meeting an elder. Similarly, an employee would offer a deeper bow to his or her boss.

• Because Japanese houses tend to be small, most entertaining is done outside the home. An invitation to someone's home, therefore, is an honor, and it is customary to bring the host a gift, such as food or liquor. And don't forget to remove your shoes at the door and put on the slippers provided.

• Business people, upon meeting for the first time always exchange business cards. When meeting with Westerners especially, Japanese businessmen refer to the cards so they can recall one's name and company position. It is also not polite to ask someone you've just met a personal question, such as "How is your family?" That's considered being nosy.

• In business, the Japanese address their co-workers by surnames, not first names, even if they have been acquainted for years.

• Dining no-nos: blowing your nose during a meal is considered disgusting. And never point with your chopsticks—it's rude.

the U.S., many American city streets shook with the noise of loud, portable stereos nicknamed ghetto blasters. With the Walkman came convenience for the user and blessed silence for everyone else.

Morita says America may be great at inventing things, but that for new ideas to be profitable the U.S. needs "the second and third types of creativity, turning products made with the new technology into a business....This exact area happens to be Japan's stronghold for the moment."

The Japanese Workplace

Japan also happens to be a model for business management. Their employees are hard-working, dependent and loyal—traits brought about in part by effective managers. The fact that the Japanese are building factories in America may be good, says journalist Bill Emmott. "If the Japanese are really better at making things than the rest of us," he says, "then getting Japanese management, organization, and technology is the fastest route to raising productivity to Japanese levels. What seems like an enormous 'rummage sale' of America's industry to the Japanese could...lead to America's salvation."

Honda, Toyota, Sony, Panasonic and many other Japanese companies now have branches in the United States where they use American workers and materials combined with Japanese management and technology. This approach benefits both countries.

Sony's Morita also notes that part of the Japanese managerial secret is that they have a true concern for their workers. Rarely is anyone ever fired in a Japanese company, and most Japanese people work for one company their entire lives.

Says Morita, "Work has more meaning to

most people than just as a means of subsistence. A Japanese worker has a sense of mission in holding his job for his lifetime as well as supporting the corporation which provides him with meaning to his life.... Repetitive hiring and firing denies any possibility of cultivating a sense of loyalty."

He says that Americans want to know how the Japanese can remain profitable if they do not fire incompetent people and retrain them instead. "I say that since a Japanese company is a community bound together by a common destiny, like the relationship between a married couple, all must work together to solve common problems." Sony of America, based in California, operates much as it does in Japan, but with American workers. Apparently the Americans at Sony are as happy and efficient as the Japanese employees. "The best thing a company can do is to treat its employees as dignified human beings," say Morita.

With loyalty comes enthusiasm and hard work. The typical Japanese worker gets up at dawn or before, depending on the length of commute, and quickly eats breakfast. Most people are at work by 8:30 sharp. Many *sarariman*, the "white collar" workers, stay at their desks until late into the evening, not wanting to go home before the boss does. Many employees do not get home before midnight. Such devotion earns paid overtime.

Other Factors In Japan's Strong Economy

As noted earlier, almost all Japanese can read and write. Education is universal. With education comes employment, and with employment, a brisk economy.

The Japanese save their money much more than Americans—roughly 15 percent of their earnings, compared to 5 percent in America.

With more money in the banks, the banks have more to lend, thus more businesses can get started or expand. For that reason, many United States economists want new tax laws which will encourage Americans to save more.

A relative lack of crime and guns and only a small drug problem means that the Japanese spend less money for police protection and related social programs. That means there is less of a drain on their economy. The same can be said for their small defense budget, which only consumes one percent of the nation's entire budget, compared to five percent in America.

And as Akio Morita notes, Japan's businesses concern themselves with producing goods rather than making money through *merger and acquisition* (where companies come together as one or a company buys another one out). This is a mania that has swept America in recent years. For example, Time, Inc. bought Warner Communications recently for $14 billion, and RJR Nabisco was purchased in the late 1980s by a group of investors for $25.4 billion. Such billion-dollar deals make the largest stockholders of the affected companies quite rich. Morita says, "Americans today make money by 'handling' money and shuffling it around instead of creating and producing goods for some actual value."

Strong For How Long?

Despite the factors already mentioned, Japan's economy is not totally worry-free. Because bank interest rates in the 1980s were low, many people took out loans—often to build businesses and to buy land. Because so many people were buying land, prices went up and up. Because prices went up, businesses that owned land appeared to be rich. Stock prices rose higher and higher.

Stocks in Japan are traded on the Tokyo Stock Exchange, much the same as stocks in New York are traded on the New York Stock Exchange. In New York, stock market rises and falls are shown on something called the *Dow Index*. In Japan, rises and falls are seen on the *Nikkei Index*.

In the first three months of 1990, the Nikkei Index dropped 28 percent. This means that the value of most Japanese stocks lost just over one-quarter of their worth, for what would be a total of $1.2 *trillion* in American money, a huge and terrible drop.

Why did this happen? The fuel of the Japanese economy was low interest rates, or put another way, cheap credit. With land prices and many other prices rising, the yen came to be worth less and less on the world market. Japanese banks raised their interest rates. Easy credit was not so easy anymore. Stock prices plummeted.

This recent turmoil raises the question of

Shopping for groceries in Japan is not much different than in America, but the Japanese consumer spends more for most goods than we do.

whether Japan will have as large of a competitive edge in world markets now that their financial markets are vulnerable and cheap credit is gone. There is no answer yet.

The drop in the Nikkei Index was not as disasterous to the world economy as many had feared. The exchange rate from yen to dollars rose, meaning it now takes more Japanese yen to buy an American dollar. For Americans, this means Japanese goods are cheaper. However, this worries economists because if Americans start buying more Japanese goods than ever, the trade imbalance will grow larger, and the American economy will grow weaker. Also, with the dollar stronger over the yen, perhaps the Japanese will not invest as much in America. Their investments, in part, have kept the American economy relatively strong.

Other economists think the Japanese will sell Japanese stocks and buy American stocks to be in the stronger stock market, which could be good for America.

Although there are no clear answers to what will happen in the future, the drop in Japan's economy shows two important things: first, Japan's economy has its weak points, and second, Japan, like the United States and many other countries, is not isolated but tied to the world in an economic partnership.

Japan's Asian Neighbors

What happens in Japan affects not only America, but the whole world. Japan's influence certainly is felt by its closest neighbors in Asia, including China and Taiwan.

These neighbors happen to have been Japanese conquests in World War II and earlier. Under the reign of Emperor Meiji (1868 to 1912), Japan defeated Russia and China in wars and took over Korea and Formosa (now called

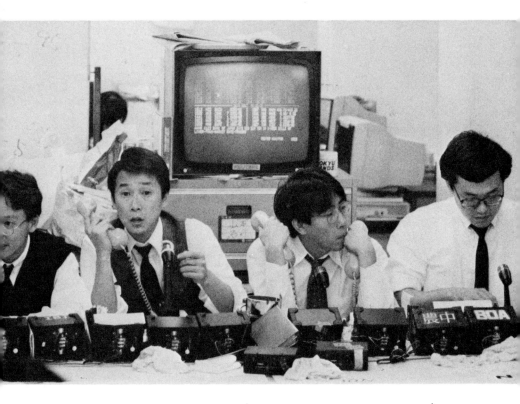

Taiwan). Japan invaded Manchuria (the north-east section of China) in 1931 and central China in 1937. By the spring of 1942, when the last defenders of the Philippines surrendered to Japan, the Japanese were on the borders of India and were within jumping range of Australia. Most of Asia was theirs until the end of the war in 1945.

Today, of course, Japan lives in relative harmony with its neighbors, but not all is perfect. Japan's economic might dominates all the other countries' economies. Japan's Asian neighbors have complaints about their own trade imbalances. Even China, a nation that tries to buy very few foreign goods, has complained about a trade imbalance.

Many of Japan's neighbors also feel that Japan isolates itself from Asia in a quest to be part of the Western world. Japanese culture has a

▲
Money traders at work in the Japanese-version of Wall Street. Japan's economy is fiercely competitive and has become the second most productive in the world.

strong Western influence in comparison to other Asian countries. Japanese diplomats felt deeply gratified by Japan's inclusion in the annual seven-power economic summit meetings of non-communist industrial nations (Great Britain, Germany, the United States, Japan, Canada, Italy, and France). Including Japan with six Western nations in such a meeting showed the Japanese people their world importance. Yet diplomats also stress that Japan must fill its international responsibilities by helping Asia.

Japan is helping out in the world on several fronts. Foreign aid is increasing yearly. In terms of giving aid to Asia, Japan is second only to the United States. On the private level, Japanese banks—the world's strongest—are becoming a major source of financing in foreign countries.

Shintaro Ishihara, co-author of *The Japan That Can Say No*, feels Japan is also helping its neighbors with know-how. "Those Asian nations where the economy has been a success story, such as Korea, Taiwan and Singapore, were all, at one time or another, under Japanese administration. We are aware that some negative things happened under the Japanese administration, but it cannot be denied that many positive changes were left behind... Entering a new era, the Pacific-Age Japan cannot remain prosperous without the rest of Asia."

Better Communication For The Future?

Perhaps the most important area that Japan needs to address for continued growth is in the area of communication—communicating with the world, or "internationalizing" itself.

Because Japan is so *homogenous* (it has few minorities), many Japanese are used to operating only within their own culture. Yet the world contains many different groups and ways of thinking, and many different ways of expressing one-self.

"Japan is not likely to exercise strong international leadership in the foreseeable future," said Harvard professor Ezra F. Vogel, author of *Japan as No. 1*. While the Japanese share a strong mutual concern for each other, says Vogel, their concerns stop at the seacoast where they block many imports in a "narrow pursuit of national self-interest."

Takashi Hosomi, head of Japan's Overseas Economic Cooperation fund in 1985, said that Japan's fundamental trouble was its inward-looking nature. "All politicians want to become vice ministers, but none of them want to become vice minister of the Foreign Ministry." If they do, they get defeated in the next election because of making global decisions that are not clearly in Japan's favor.

Even Akio Morita agrees: "One of the reasons why U.S.-Japan relations are in such a mess is that Japan has not told the U.S. the things that need to be said." The point he stresses in *The Japan That Can Say No* is that the Japanese tend to say "well" or "probably" when they really mean "no." Saying "no" will permit the two sides to understand each other more clearly and work on solutions that much sooner.

"Living in a homogenous society since childhood," Morita says, "we Japanese have grown up without practical experience in quarreling and fighting in a heterocultural [many races] environment.... Wordless communication and telepathy will just not happen."

Robert J. Samuelson, an American economist, said that what America and Japan have in common are delusions. "The American delusion is that competition from Japanese trade and investment threatens our well being." In fact, the competition has made our companies more efficient

Japan's Mount Fuji is an inspiring sight.

and imaginative, improving our standard of living. In the 1980s, factory productivity (output per hour) in the United States jumped 38 percent.

"The Japanese delusion is that all foreign criticism is sour grapes," said Samuelson. They take American criticism hard because since the war, the U.S. has been the country against which Japan relentlessly measures itself. With what they see as Japan bashing, the Japanese then bash back. This is not good for communications.

All in all, Japan remains a very important country in the world culturally, spiritually, and economically. In this day of the FAX, electronic mail, express services, satellite phone calls and speedy transportation, the world is more connected than it ever has been. No longer can countries stand totally on their own, isolated. Each country is dependent on others. Therefore, open trade, a lack of discrimination, and healthy communication are mandatory in order for all to prosper. Each country is a world partner.

Glossary

BESUBORU. Baseball, one of the most popular team sports in Japan.

BUDDHISM. One of two national religions of Japan; the other is Shintoism.

BUNRAKU. Japanese puppet theater.

CHA-NO-YU. Name for the time-honored Japanese tea ceremony.

DIET. The Japanese Parliament.

HAIKU. A poem; the precise 17-syllable length of a *haiku* is unique to Japanese literature.

IKEBANA. The classical Japanese art of flower arranging.

KABUKI. Colorful Japanese theater featuring song and dance.

NIKKEI INDEX. The Japanese stock exchange.

NOH. A style of Japanese theater with only two actors, who usually wear face masks.

PACHINKO. Japanese-style pinball game.

PRIME MINISTER. The highest elected official in Japan.

SARARIMAN. Japanese term closest in meaning to American "white collar" workers.

SHINTOISM. One of two national religions in Japan; the other is Buddhism.

SHOGUNATE. In the middle ages, this was the name for Japan's form of military government.

TRADE IMBALANCE. When a country imports more than it exports, it has a trade imbalance or trade *deficit*.

TRADE SURPLUS. When a country exports more than it imports, it has a trade surplus.

WA. A Japanese word that refers to team spirit; the pride and interest of the group above that of the individual.

BIBLIOGRAPHY

Fields, George. *From Bonsai to Levis.* New York, New American Library, 1983

Hillenbrand, Barry. "Wa is Hell." *Time,* September 25, 1989

Jameson, Sam. "Japan: From the Rubble a Renaissance." *Los Angeles Times,* August 6, 1985
—"Japan Torn Between Pacifism, Defense." *Los Angeles Times,* August 7, 1985
—"Japanese Still Have Few Friends in Asia." *Los Angeles Times,* August 8, 1985

Maraimi, Fosco. *Tokyo.* Amsterdam, Time-Life Books, 1976

Morita, Akio and Shintaro Ishihara. *The Japan That Can Say No.* Kobunsha, Kappa-Holmes, 1989

Powell, Bill and Bradley Martin. "What Japan Thinks of Us." *Newsweek,* April 2, 1990

Reischauer, Edwin O. *The Japanese.* Cambridge, Harvard University Press, 1978

Rowen, Hobart. "Subtle Shift of Power in Group of 7." *The Washington Post,* April 22, 1990

Seidensticker, Edward and the Editors of Life. *Japan.* New York, Time Incorporated, 1962
Schoenberger, Karl. "For Japan, Gilded Age of Riches." *Los Angeles Times,* January 30, 1989

Time-Life. *Japan*. New York, Time-Life Books, 1985

Wolferen, Karel van. *The Enigma of Japanese Power*. New York, Alfred A. Knopf, 1989

Index

Picture Credits

Map from MAPS ON FILE.
  Copyright 1981 by Martin
  Greenwald Associates.
  Reprinted with the permission
  of Facts On File, Inc.,
  New York   9

AP/Wide World Photos, Inc.   11, 21, 24, 27,
    28, 30-31, 33, 39,
    40, 43, 49, 51, 54

Peter Arnold, Inc.   16, 37